Living Jewels

THE NATURAL DESIGN OF BEETLES

Poul Beckmann

Introduction by Ruth Kaspin

Prestel

Munich · London · New York

We would like to express our appreciation to Mr Jürgen Tesch,
publisher at Prestel, for sharing our enthusiasm, helping us to refine the design
of this book, and for giving us the opportunity to realize our first
publication. We are most grateful to our editor, Ms Philippa Hurd,
for her help in creating what we hope will be an intriguing and enjoyable
introduction to the realm of the beetles;
and to Mr Matthias Hauer for his elegant design.

We dedicate this book to our dearest and most appreciative audience, our mothers,
Amelia Bech Nielsen and Rebecca Kaspin, and to the memory of our fathers,
Arnold Beckmann and Solomon Kaspin.

© Prestel-Verlag, Munich, London, New York 2001
© for text and illustrations by Poul and Ruth Beckmann

The right of Poul and Ruth Beckmann to be identified
as authors of this work has been asserted in accordance
with the Copyright, Designs and Patents Act 1988.

Prestel-Verlag
Mandlstrasse 26 · D-80802 Munich
Tel.: (89) 38-17-09-0 · Fax: (89) 38-17-09-35
www.prestel.de

4 Bloomsbury Place · London · WC1A 2QA
Tel.: (020) 7323 5004 · Fax: (020) 7636 8004

175 Fifth Avenue, Suite 402 · New York · NY 10010
Tel.: (212) 995 2720 · Fax: (212) 995 2733
www.prestel.com

Library of Congress Control Number: 2001092038

Prestel books are available worldwide.
Please contact your nearest bookseller
or any of the above addresses for information
concerning your local distributor.

Editorial direction: Philippa Hurd
Design and production: Matthias Hauer, Munich

Typeface: Bodoni Old Face by G.G. Lange
Origination: phg, Martinsried
Printing: Sellier Druck, Freising
Binding: Conzella, Pfarrkirchen

Printed in Germany
on acid-free paper

ISBN 3-7913-2528-0

CONTENTS

Introduction
by Ruth Kaspin
6

The Plates
13

Beetle Profiles
109

Selected Bibliography
112

INTRODUCTION

This book is a visual feast of beetles; its purpose is to introduce some amazing creatures who, for the most part, lead their lives and go about their business unseen. Due to their diminutive size, the majority of beetles fly under the radar of human notice. The immature phases of their life cycles are spent hidden in the soil or within layers of tree bark or in the roots of plants. The adult portion of their lives is usually brief, confined to a single season.

The order of Coleoptera—the beetles—has evolved over 230 million years. Shaping themselves to fit every conceivable climate and landscape on earth, they have developed a phantasmagorical diversity of shapes and sizes, colors, patterns, and textures. In the beetle's natural world his fabulous decoration is the camouflage that allows him to blend seamlessly into the leaf litter of the forest floor or the shiny foliage of the rainforest canopy. Bark-like texture allows a longhorn beetle to disappear on a branch; patterning on a flower beetle mimics dappled sunlight and shadow through leaves. When lifted out of the concealing clutter their beauty comes into vivid focus. They are presented here, magnified and isolated against stark white backgrounds, to allow for a close inspection and appreciation of their complex structures, varieties of form, and kaleidoscope of colors and patterns.

With 350,000 identified species within 166 families, beetles represent one in five living species on earth, and one in four of all animal species. Any attempt to show them all would be an impossible task. This collection cannot come close to being a true representative sampling of all beetles, or all beetle families; it is merely a showcase of a few of the most beautiful and most readily available to collectors. Nor is this book an entomology text. Given that the subject is so enormous and diverse, scientific treatments are necessarily very specific, with volumes devoted to data concerning a single genus or species. The aim of this book is to present a small sample from the vast array of beetle beauty, a natural gallery encompassing forms ranging from the adorable to the grotesque.

Within the universe of beetle variety lies an encyclopedic vocabulary of ornament, a vast visual territory to be explored. As conditions and habitats change, whether by human intervention or forces of nature, beetles continue to evolve. They are nature's most prolific unending design project, and a limitless resource for artists, artisans, and designers.

BEETLE VARIETIES

Beetles inhabit every continent on earth except Antarctica. In the temperate zones of the world, wider seasonal temperature variations result in less species diversity, but more individuals per species. In the tropics, where climate is more consistent year round, there is an enormous diversity of species, but with fewer individuals per species. Beetles thrive in tropical, temperate, and subarctic forests. There are aquatic beetles and desert-dwelling beetles. Beetles inhabit grassy savannahs, suburban backyards, and kitchen pantries. In short, they are virtually everywhere, and their myriad sizes, shapes, and colors reflect their diverse habitats and ways of life.

In size, beetles range from the tiniest of the feather beetles, barely one quarter of a millimeter in length, to *Titanus giganteus*, a cerambycid, or long-horn, of the Amazon basin, which can be as long as 20 centimeters. Other beetle behemoths whose names reflect their impressive size include the South American Dynastids, hercules and elephant beetles, several Asian Dynastids called atlas beetles, and the African goliath beetles. Individuals among these species can reach lengths of between 11 and 15 centimeters.

Beetle body form varies considerably from family to family. Cerambycids are the long-horned beetles, so called because their antennae can be as long as their bodies and often dramatically longer. The superfamily Scarabaeoidea is the easy winner of the prize for the most astonishing arrays of horns, crests, spikes, prongs, and protuberances. The configurations of these remarkable ornaments vary widely among the families and species, ranging from species with a single horn curving forward from the head, to species with horns and spines jutting forward from the thorax, framing backward thrusting head-horns, paired or single, in varieties of curves, bifurcations, and serrations. If these horned grotesques are the stuff of nightmares, then weevils are surely the comic relief. Colloquially called "snout beetles", weevils, typically, have narrow, elongated heads and a sort of stoop-shouldered splayed-legged stance.

THE COLOR OF BEETLES

Beetles are invertebrates, which means that they have no internal skeletons. A tough, yet flexible exoskeleton called the cuticle serves as their structural support. The cuticle serves the dual purpose of skeleton and skin, armature and protective coating. It is composed of protein and chitin, a tough, fibrous substance related to cellulose. Layers of chitin function like natural fiberglass, combining toughness and flexibility with the added advantage, for a flying creature, of being extremely light.

Coloration in beetles comes either from pigmentation or optical interference or both factors in combination. Pigmentation results from the presence of melanins, producing browns and blacks; or carotenoids, producing reds, oranges, and yellows. Optical interference colors result when light reflecting and refracting through the micro-thin transparent outer layer of the cuticle interacts visually with the pigmented layer beneath. The final effect is iridescence, in some cases subtle and lustrous, in others metallic and flashy. The mechanics of optical interference produce a variable, fluctuating color, like the moiré rainbows on the surface of a diffraction grating. Light wrapping the contours of the beetle's body produces color shifts; a green surface graduates to a pink or magenta edge, deep greens and blues flash bronze or gold reflections. With the added dimension of textures such as ridges, ribbing, granulation, or dimpling, the play of light over the surface creates ever more nuances and variations in color. Patterning in beetles includes all variations of stripes, zig-zags, chevrons, pinstripes, freeform brushstrokes, spots, dots, blotches, and mottling.

Many of the taxonomic names which categorize beetles within their respective genera and species are almost poetic, revealing that their human namers' scientific objectivity came tinged with an appreciation of the beauty of these creatures. Translated from the Latin, *Euchroma* means beautiful color; *Chrysophora*, gold bearer; *Chrysochroa*, with a golden surface; and *Sumptuosa gemma* means sumptuous, costly, and gemlike.

Many beetles exhibit cryptic coloration—their color allows them to disappear into their surroundings. Given the tremendous diversity of beetle habitats, beetle camouflage includes quite a variety of colors and textures. Iridescent and metallic colors are commonest in the tropical rainforests of Southeast Asia, South America, and Australia, while in African grasslands pigment colors in red, orange, yellow, and brown predominate.

Some of the most exotic and beautiful examples of iridescence are to be found in the various genera within the family Buprestidae, the metallic wood-boring beetles. They are commonly known as jewel beetles or flying jewels, entirely appropriate names, as no other creatures so closely approximate the color and glitter of precious gems. The elytra (wing sheaths) of Amazonian buprestids are strung and worn as necklaces and ear pendants, and fashioned into headdresses by indigenous tribes in South America.

In Japan there exists a buprestid beetle shrine, the Tamamushi-no-zushi in the Horyuji temple at Nara. Built in the seventh century AD for the Empress Suiko, it contains sacred Buddhist objects embellished with nine thousand shimmering green elytra of the buprestid *Chrysochroa fulgidissima* set in gilded filigree. An old Japanese legend says that a specimen of *Chrysochroa* placed in a tansu chest will cause clothing to magically accumulate within.

Ranging in size from 1.5 to 70 mm, buprestid beetles are usually spindle-shaped, rather like an aerodynamic elongated almond with rounded head and thorax, and abdomen tapering down to a point. Resembling nothing so much as a Surrealist's vision of a toothbrush, some buprestids of the genus *Julodis* sport bundles of setae (bristle-like structures) in vivid shades of yellow or orange, contrasting with their metallic blue or green bodies. Another buprestid genus, *Sternocera*, has the same overall almond shape. Their colors vary by continent with a number of Southeast Asian species being entirely metallic emerald green in color, while some Indian and Sri Lankan cousins contrast a metallic green head and thorax with deep plum red elytra. Central African species display rich earth reds, cinnabar, golden ochre, and shiny black.

A number of ruteline scarabs of the genus *Chrysina* have coloration that is utterly unique among living creatures. Their colors are such that they appear to be made of polished metal. Some golden, some silver, and some two-toned, with golden thorax and silver elytra, they are highly prized by collectors. Native to Costa Rica, and rare enough to be protected species, these specimens are costly and difficult to obtain.

BEETLE MAGIC AND MYSTICISM

Ornaments in the shape of beetles have been found which date back twenty-five thousand years to the early Magdalenian era. Fashioned from anthracite, a hard form of coal, they were highly polished and drilled with a hole, presumably so that they could by strung and worn.

Beetles, especially the scarab, inspired creation myths in many ancient cultures. Little sparkling beings crowned with horns flying in the air or materializing mysteriously from underground, they must have been objects of fascination and awe. In the ancient imagination, everything in nature had a magic purpose and meaning. In an aboriginal South American creation myth, undoubtedly inspired by the dung rolling scarabs, a great Creator beetle models man and woman from clay. A similar ancient Sumatran myth tells of a great beetle flying down from the sky bearing a ball of matter to form the earth.

The image of the scarab with his wings spread, clutching the solar disc between his claws is a universally familiar icon. As well known as the pyramids or King Tutankhamun's golden deathmask, it is emblematic of Ancient Egypt. No insect has ever attained a status comparable to the revered position given by the Egyptians to the scarab: for thirty centuries, the scarab was venerated as the personification of rebirth and immortality.

Much of the mysticism associated with beetles derives from their life cycle, which begins in the earth, hidden from human view. *Scarabaeus sacer*, the sacred scarab, tunnels into the earth to create nurseries for its eggs. It furnishes each underground chamber with a ball of animal dung which will serve as food for the hatching larvae. In the curious antics of the beetle, head down, propelling itself backward, rolling a ball of dung with its hind legs, the Egyptians saw a representation of their universe in microcosm. The beetle, emerging from the earth, rolling its ball, seemed to mirror the spectacle of the sun god Ra, rolling the ball of the sun across the sky. The sun sets, sinking below the horizon, and likewise, the scarab disappears into the earth, but both sun and scarab will rise, reborn. The Egyptian name for the scarab, *cheper*, derives from the same root as the word for becoming or "coming into being". Chepri, the god of creation, one of the avatars of Ra, was shown, alternately, with a scarab above his head, or with a scarab in place of a human head.

It has been postulated that the practice of mummifying the dead may have been inspired by the metamorphosis of the scarab. The pupa is the cocoon-like stage wherein the larval beetle accomplishes its maturation; it is a period of development and change within, but its outward appearance is inert, as a corpse. The emergence of a live, adult beetle from a seemingly inanimate husk was dramatic evidence of the beetle's mystical ability to return from the netherworld. Perhaps the ancient priests reasoned that encasing the dead in protective pupa-like wrappings might similarly serve the dead on their sojourn in the afterlife and ensure a glorious rebirth.

Scarabs rendered in green stones such as basalt, schist, or jade were placed over the hearts of the mummified dead. Suspended on gold chains or wires, and sometimes inscribed with passages from the Book of the Dead, these "heart scarabs" were to serve as proxies for the hearts of the deceased when they were called before the tribunal in the underworld, to ensure that the heart would not bear witness against its owner.

Over the course of three millennia, untold numbers of scarab amulets were made in a variety of semi-precious stones, faience, soapstone, and ivory, and worn by people at all levels of society. The wealthy and powerful wore them mounted in elaborately worked gold rings, armbands, and pectorals while a peasant might wear a single scarab strung on cord. The pharoahs issued commemorative scarabs bearing inscriptions detailing the momentous events of their reigns.

Egyptian civilization, at its height, extended its cultural influence throughout the Mediterranean region and, in the Near East, as far as the Euphrates valley, and thus the wearing of scarabs as amulets or good luck charms spread throughout the ancient world. With the passage of time, some of their symbolic attributes were forgotten and others took their place. As the Egyptians had always believed all scarabs to be male, the scarab was a totem of masculinity, and Egyptian soldiers wore them into battle. Adopted as a mascot by Roman soldiers the wearing of a scarab as an amulet spread throughout the Roman empire.

Some of the earliest Christian sects equated the scarab as a symbol of rebirth with the resurrection of Christ, but, the majority of Christian belief associated the scarab with filth and degradation, and the scarab became the symbol of the sinner. Throughout the Middle Ages the foundation of all knowledge of natural history was the *Physiologus*, an ancient Greek text whose origin is believed to be second century Alexandria. Translated into Latin, and subsequently into almost all of the European languages, it was a compilation of descriptions of animals, both real and fantastic, with the emphasis on their symbolic and spiritual attributes. According to the *Physiologus*, the scarab was a creature formed from excrement, spending its life in filth, and creating its offspring from dung:

> the dung beetles are the heretics, defiled with the stench of heresy…
> the balls of dung…which they roll back and forth on the ground are evil
> thoughts and heresies, which have been created out of wickedness and foulness.

Old European folklore is full of superstition centered around beetles. The stag beetle was believed to be capable of carrying burning embers in its jaws and was held responsible for setting houses on fire. A French peasant would kill a stag beetle to ward off bad luck, while in Bavaria the head of the beetle would be carried as a good luck charm, capable of attracting wealth. In some countries the head or mandibles were worn as charms to ward off the evil eye. The dor beetle, a relative of the sacred scarab, was called "the Devil's Steed" in ancient Greece, and its reputation for possessing supernatural powers continued on in European folk wisdom. A dor beetle stranded on its back had to be rescued. Anyone passing by who chose to ignore its plight risked having his house struck by lightning or his crops destroyed by hailstorms. The dor beetle was also thought to possess the power to attract wealth—a dor beetle placed in a money chest would ensure a perpetual supply of gold.

BEETLES BEFORE THE BAR

Beetles' survival strategies have been perfected over millions of years of evolution and their various species have been extremely successful in propagating themselves in enormous numbers. Unfortunately, beetle success and human success have, occasionally, been at cross-purposes, and beetles have been called upon to account for their behavior.

The origins of animal trials go back at least as far as the classical period of Greece. According to Plato, if an animal killed a man, the relatives of the deceased were required to file formal charges against the offending beast. The ensuing trial invariably produced a guilty verdict and an execution. Proceedings against domestic animals were civil matters, and, with the passage of time, the incidence of executions decreased in cases involving more valuable animals.

Medieval animal trials were convened in both the civil and ecclesiastical courts. The ecclesiastical courts were not involved in cases of transgressions by individual domestic animals. Their jurisdiction was in cases in which classes of creatures such as rats, mice, grasshoppers or other "vermin" appeared in large enough numbers to constitute a threat to the health and well-being of the human community.

Cockchafers, melolonthine scarabs, were present in medieval Europe in numbers that sometimes reached plague proportions. A graphic illustration is chronicled in a sixteenth-century account of a swarm of cockchafers which fell into a river and, by the enormity of their number, completely clogged a water mill, bringing the mill wheel to a stop. In this case, a considerable number of hungry birds saved the day. Adult cockchafers do not cause damage to food crops; their larvae, however, are veritable eating machines capable of devastating a community's food supply.

The first recorded ecclesiastical proceedings against cockchafers, or, more accurately, against cockchafer larvae, took place in 1320, in Avignon. Preliminary to the trial, two priests in ceremonial garb visited the affected land and proclaimed a summons to all larval cockchafers to appear before the Bishop, with failure to appear punishable by excommunication. Written notice of the summons was posted, which included advice to the larvae of their right to court-appointed counsel. When the defendants failed to appear, their advocate presented the defense that his clients, as fellow beings of God's creation, had the right to seek food, and that their failure to appear was the result of not having been guaranteed the customary safe passage to and from the trial. The ultimate resolution of the case was that the larvae were to quit the disputed territory in exchange for a plot of land that the court deemed sufficient for their needs. Any individuals who failed to relocate were declared outlaws, and, as such, could be exterminated. In a similar trial in 1478, in Lausanne, Switzerland, the unfortunate larvae did not fare quite so well: they were declared excommunicate by the Bishop.

BEETLE JEWELS

Beetle wings have been used for centuries as jewelry or embellishment on clothing and decorative objects. Beetles have two pairs of wings: the tough, chitinous forward pair, the elytra, fold down over most of the beetle's body forming a protective case over the more fragile flight wings. In flight, they are held open and angled to create additional aerodynamic lift as the flight wings function. Durable, virtually weightless, and spectacular in color, beetle elytra are ideal natural jewels.

The most extensive use of beetle elytra in textiles was in the Mogul culture of Jaipur in India. Existing samples of clothing and accessories embellished with beetle wings date back to the seventeenth and eighteenth centuries. The emerald green elytra were worked onto fabrics with metallic thread in a method similar to the way a cabochon stone is secured in a bezel setting. Beetle elytra as a commodity were harvested by the millions in the hardwood forests of Burma for export to India. In the rainy season the beetles swarm in search of mates. After mating has occurred and the eggs have been laid, the adult beetles die, making the harvesting of the wings a simple matter of gathering up the dead insects. In the nineteenth century a new export market developed for textiles with beetle-wing decoration. Victorian England had a fascination for exotic goods from the far-flung corners of the Empire and so an industry developed with Indian artisans producing textiles, fans, and other decorative accessories for export to England and the rest of Europe.

The Victorian taste for the exotic intersected with the heightened interest in the natural sciences inspired by the investigations of Charles Darwin and Sir Alfred Russel Wallace. The collecting of minerals, plants, and exotic insect specimens became common pastimes. No Victorian parlor was complete without a collection of beautiful tropical butterflies or beetles, mounted under glass. Victorian ladies took up the fashion of wearing live jewel beetles tethered by tiny golden chains. Jewelry was made which incorporated beetle elytra or from the entire bodies of buprestid or chrysomelid beetles.

Ornaments incorporating beetle elytra, femurs, horns, and mandibles are worn in aboriginal societies throughout the Amazon Basin, in New Guinea, and among the hill tribes in Thailand and Burma. All of these ornaments, in addition to their obvious beauty, are thought to possess some of the beetle's spiritual energy. More elaborate ritual ornaments are fashioned as objects of power to be worn only by certain members of the society in the performance of ceremonies designed to attract and "possess" the magical attributes of the beetle. Such objects and garments are handled with extreme care, as their misuse has the potential to bring about disaster.

In some areas of India and Sri Lanka the jewel buprestid *Chrysochroa ocellata* does double duty as a pet and as a brooch. Large, at about four centimeters in length, and metallic green with coppery red flashes, *Chrysochroa* is worn as jewelry on festive occasions. The beetle is tethered to a tiny chain pinned to the clothing. Beads, rhinestones, and bits of chain are glued to the shells of live zopherid beetles native to Mexico and Central America, and they too, are worn as living jewels.

The Louvre in Paris possesses a vast collection of Egyptian antiquities, thanks, in large part to Napoleon's Egyptian campaigns at the end of the eighteenth century. The early nineteenth century was the beginning of the widespread use of ancient Egyptian motifs in modern Western fashion and design. Egyptian-inspired furniture, textiles, and jewelry bore somewhat Europeanized versions of sphinxes, representations of the goddess Isis, the stylized lotus, and, of course, the scarab. Nineteenth-century archaeological expeditions in the Mediterranean and Near East and the construction of the Suez Canal between 1859 and 1869 kept European and American fascination for the region alive.

The sheer abundance of their production in the ancient world left multitudes of scarabs to be found. In addition to those of Egyptian origin, the popularity of the scarab in ancient Carthage led to the establishment of workshops in Sardinia devoted solely to their manufacture. Scarabs of Minoan origin bore the favorite design motif of Crete, the labyrinth, engraved on their reverse surface. Many nineteenth-century jewels incorporate authentic antique scarabs.

In 1922 the archeologist Howard Carter discovered the tomb of King Tutankhamun. In the year that elapsed between the initial opening of the tomb and the discovery of the chamber containing the King's golden sarcophagus, ancient Egyptian symbols and motifs had, once again, become the reigning fad and fashion in Europe and America, and the inspiration for yet another generation of artists and designers.

Scarabs have been rendered in fine gold and precious stones, enamels, art glass and hardstone by all the major jewelry designers of the nineteenth and twentieth centuries. Louis C. Tiffany's personal collection of ancient scarabs was the inspiration for his scarabs of iridescent glass. Many of Cartier's jewels incorporated antique Egyptian scarabs. The stylized geometry of the ancient scarabs was equally at home set within the sinuous curves of Art Nouveau or set off by the sophisticated geometry of the Art Deco style. The scarab possesses an irresistible charisma, even to the modern imagination. Whenever an important collection of Egyptian antiquities is assembled for an international touring exhibition, the world of design experiences another Egyptian revival, and the scarab rises again.

BEETLE COLLECTING AS A HOBBY

There is probably no such person as a casual beetle collector. Whether a collector hunts for his specimens in the wild or purchases them from dealers, the building of a collection, once begun, becomes a passion. Given the number of beetle species, there is virtually no danger of a collection ever being "complete". Even if one already owns a specimen of a particular species, there is always the possibility of finding another specimen that is slightly larger, or whose color has a slightly different nuance, or whose pattern is finer, or bolder, or whose horns are spikier, jaws larger, or antennae longer. Collections can be wide-ranging or specialized. Some collectors concentrate on a single family, others look for beetle beauties or beetle grotesques throughout the families. Some specialize in the biggest of the big. Still others hunt close to home for regional native species.

Attending an insect fair is an ideal introduction to collecting. Many museums, zoos, and universities sponsor insect fairs which feature displays of private collections, live exotic insects, and dealers selling insect specimens and equipment for collecting and preparing specimens. A number of international entomological fairs, such as the annual fairs in Frankfurt and Tokyo, attract dealers and collectors from all nations who buy, sell, and trade specimens. But the most obvious place to begin a collection involves an expedition to your own backyard.

Charles Darwin was an avid beetle collector. It has even been suggested that his fascination for beetles was, at least in part, a motivating factor in his choice of natural science as his vocation. In his autobiography, reminiscing on his student days at Cambridge, he recalls beetle collecting as his most enjoyable pursuit:

> I will give a proof of my zeal: one day, on tearing off some old bark, I saw two rare beetles, and seized one in each hand; then I saw a third and new kind, which I could not bear to lose, so that I popped the one which I held in my right hand into my mouth. Alas! it ejected some intensely acrid fluid, which burnt my tongue so that I was forced to spit the beetle out, which was lost, as was the third one.

A responsible collector must respect the protected or endangered status of certain insect species. A number of nations have restrictions or outright bans on the export of rare native fauna. Those species which are naturally numerous in the world, combined with many captive breeding programs, provide more than enough variety to satisfy any beetle enthusiast.

BEETLE PETS

Interest in beetles is not confined to the collecting of dead specimens. In some parts of the world, beetles are kept as pets. In Japan, stag beetles, members of the family Lucanidae, and superfamily Scarabaeoidea, are as popular as dogs or cats in the West. Stag beetles are quite long-lived. They spend several years in the larval stage and their adult lives range from three to five years.

The depletion of forest habitats in Japan has made many wild beetle species difficult to find, but this does not present a problem to the prospective pet owner. One has only to take a field trip to a department store or pet shop to find, not only live beetles, but all of the supplies necessary to make a beetle's life healthy and comfortable. Store shelves are stocked with packaged foods, dietary supplements, and the various types of decayed, processed wood chips that double as nesting material and nutrition for hatching larvae. Manufacturers and processors of beetle supplies are numerous and quite competitive in advertising the superior quality of their products. There are about thirty varieties of stag beetles native to Japan. About a dozen species are raised commercially to be sold as pets. An affordable choice, at about $10, is the stag beetle *Prosopocoilus inclinatus*, a favorite among children.

Ookuwagata is the Japanese name for *Dorcus curvidens*, considered the most desirable of beetle pets. In the mid-1990s, beetle-keeping attained a fad status, with a record-sized 78 millimeter *Dorcus* male fetching the equivalent of $20,000. The furore has since subsided and prices now average about $80 for an adult male of ordinary size, with extraordinarily large specimens costing as much as several thousand dollars.

The relative sparseness of wild populations of these beetles is not a matter of concern in Japan. Indeed because of the nationwide popularity of beetle-rearing as a hobby, these species are not threatened with extinction.

# The Plates

1

Stephanorrhina guttata

Gymnetis hyperoglyphica obscura / Gymnetis flavomarginata sallei

Euchroea histrionica

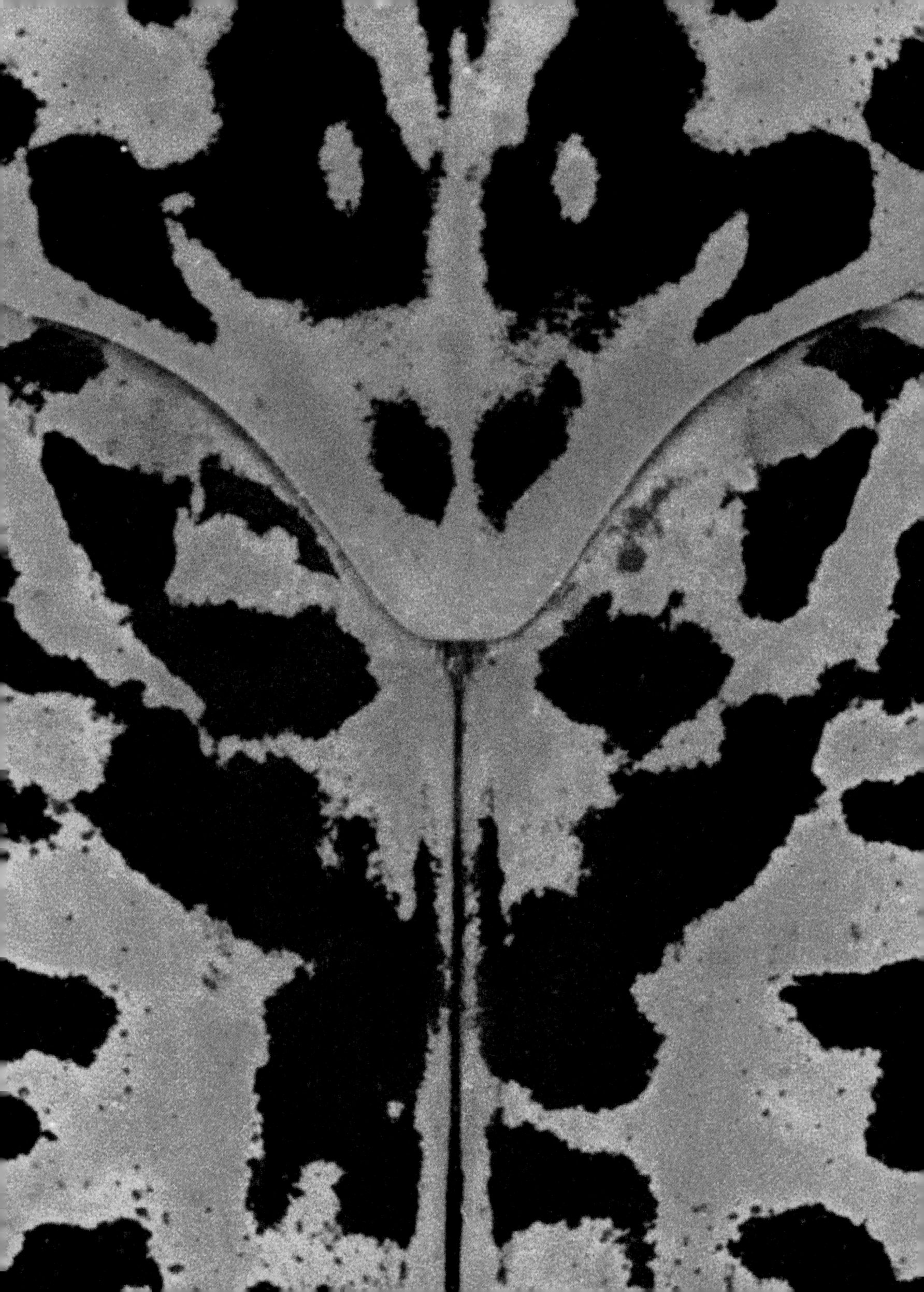

Gymnetis pantherina

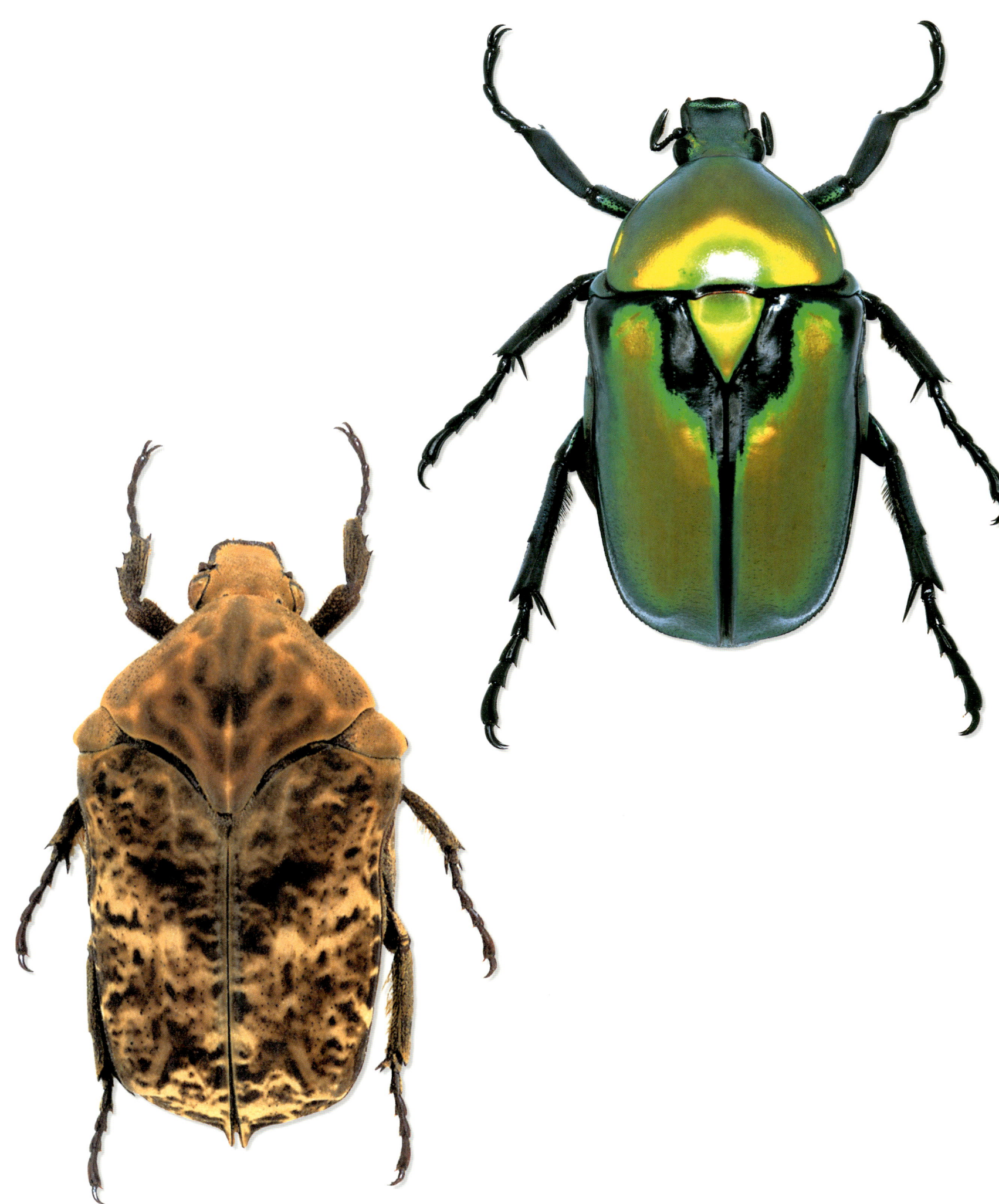

Gymnetis flaveola / Rhomborrhina resplendens

6
Gymnetis stellata

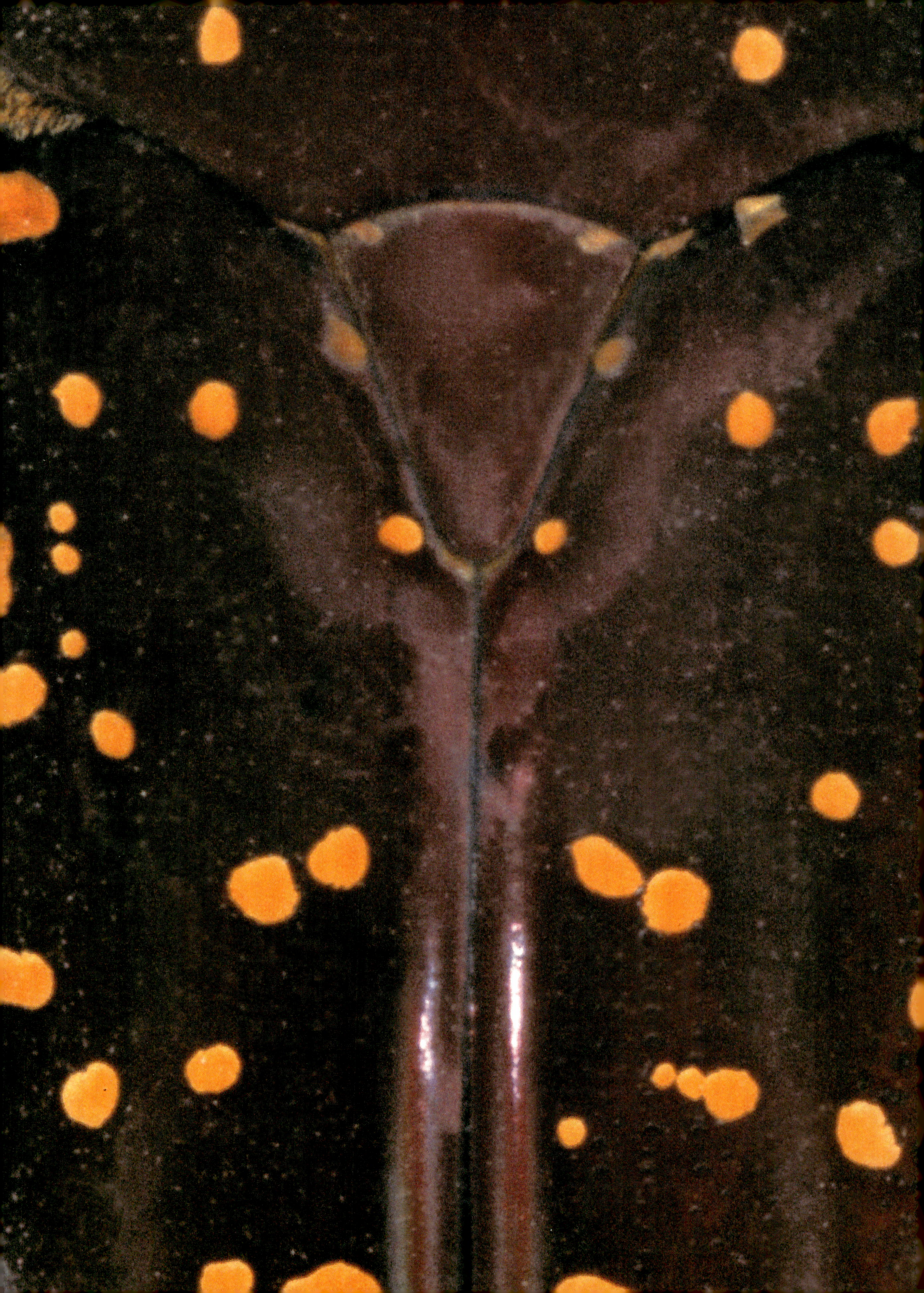

7
Celedota splendens

Phaedimus jagori

9
Theodosia perakensis

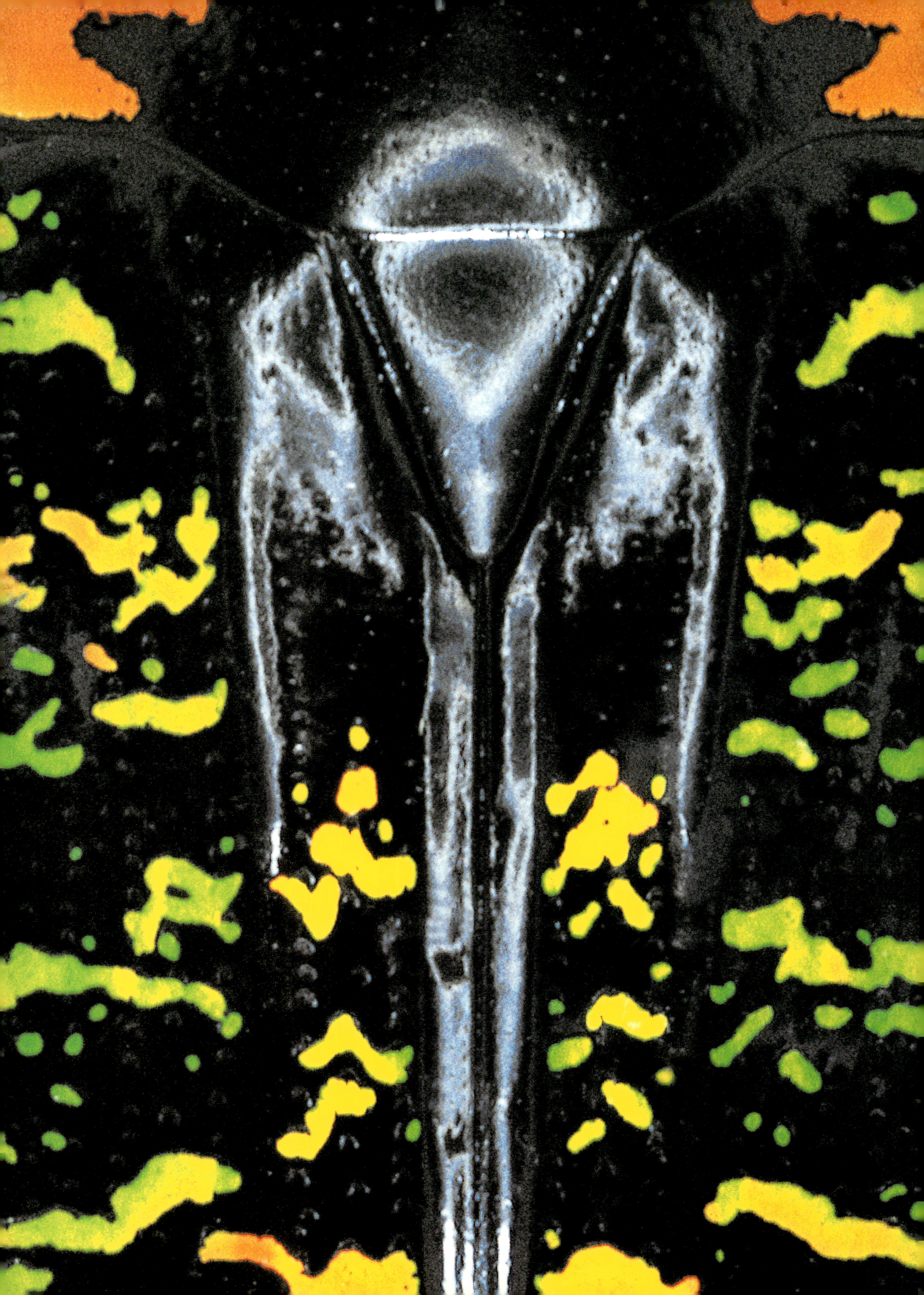

10

Euchroea clementi

11

Euchroea vadoni

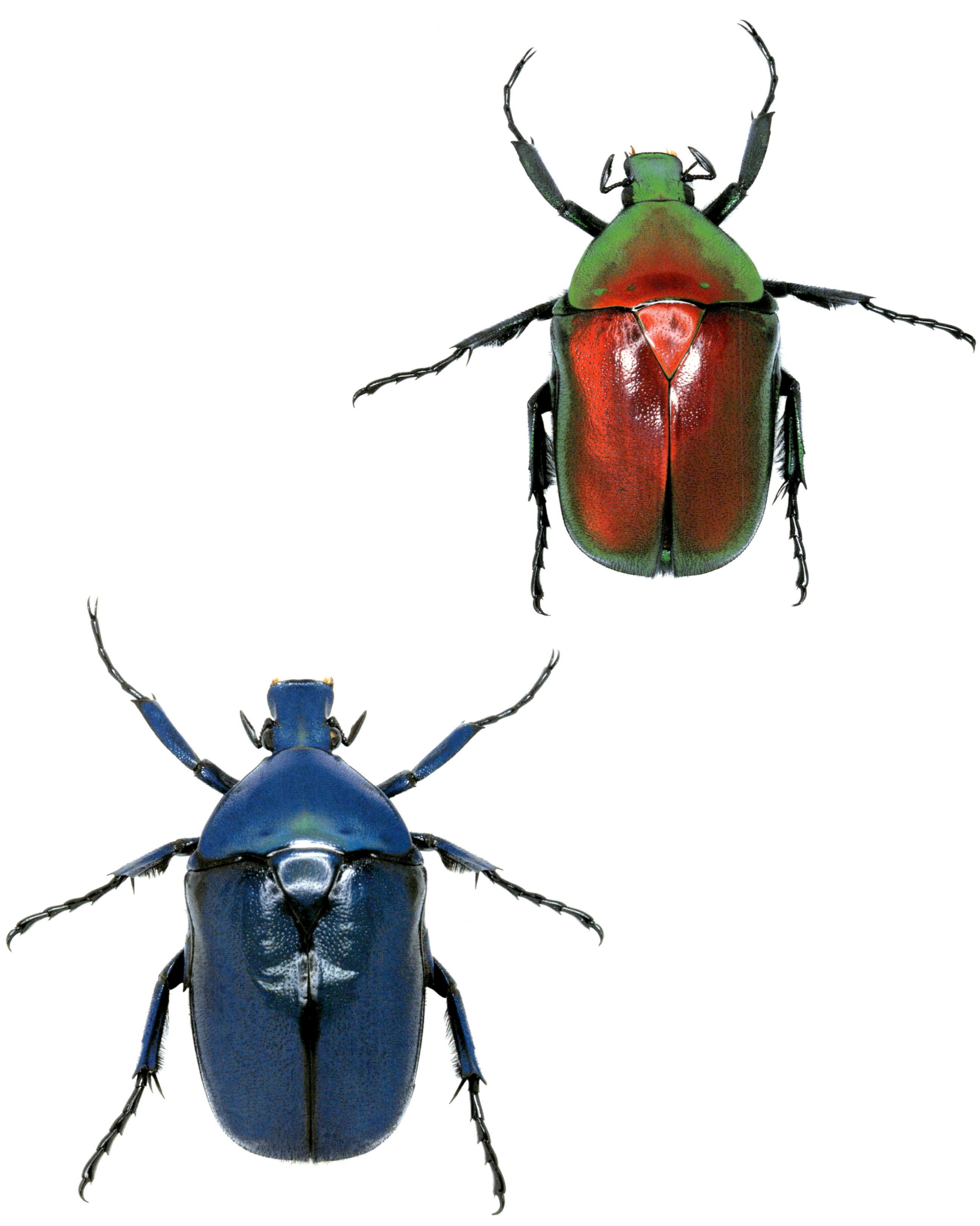

Torynorrhina flammea

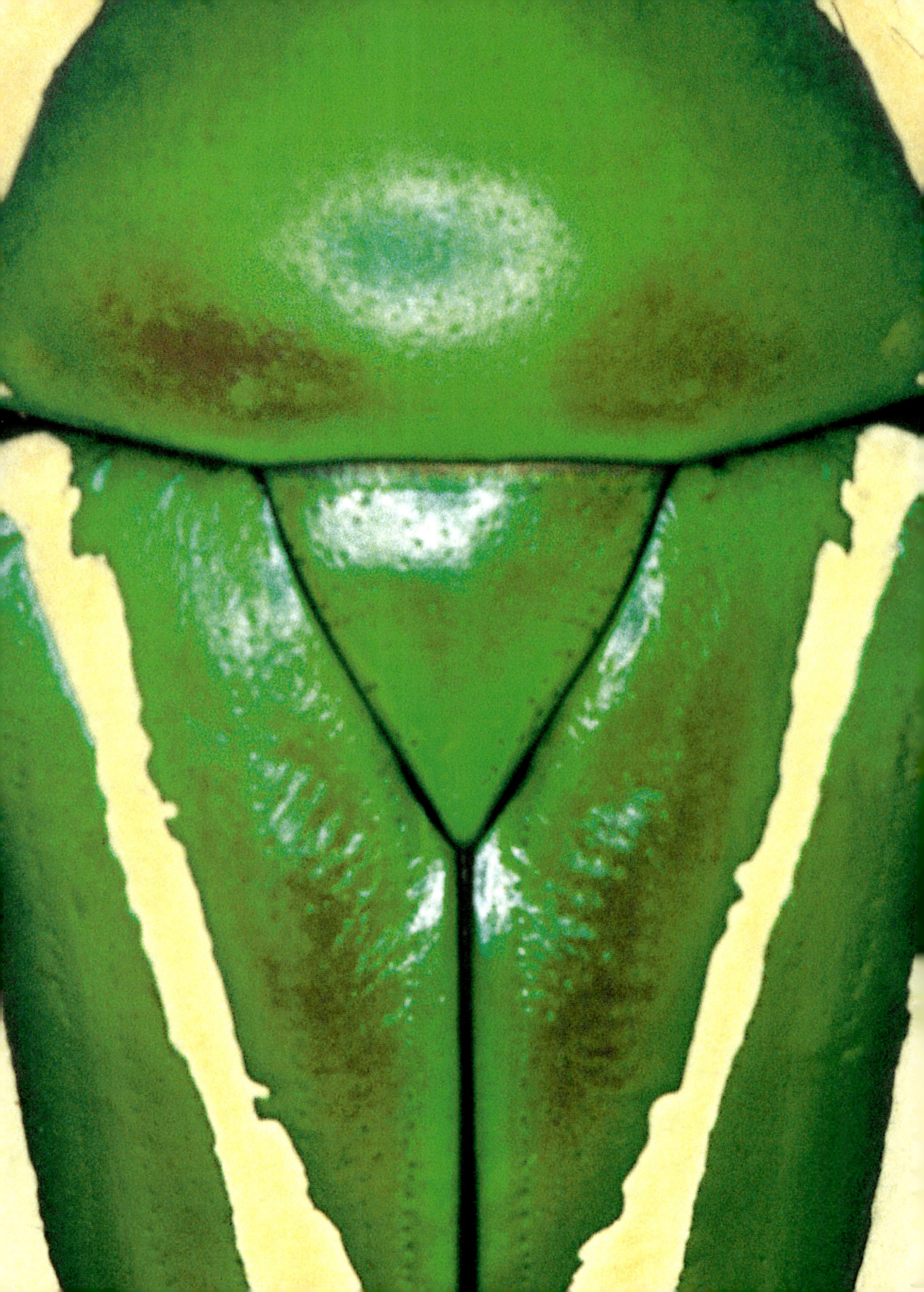

Dicranorrhina derbyana

Steirastoma marmoratus / Steirastoma brevis

15

Xylorhiza adusta

16

Arrhenotus raphaelae

17
Euryphagus lundii

Rosalia alpina

19
Plinthocoelium suavoleus plicayum

20

Rhagium sycophanta

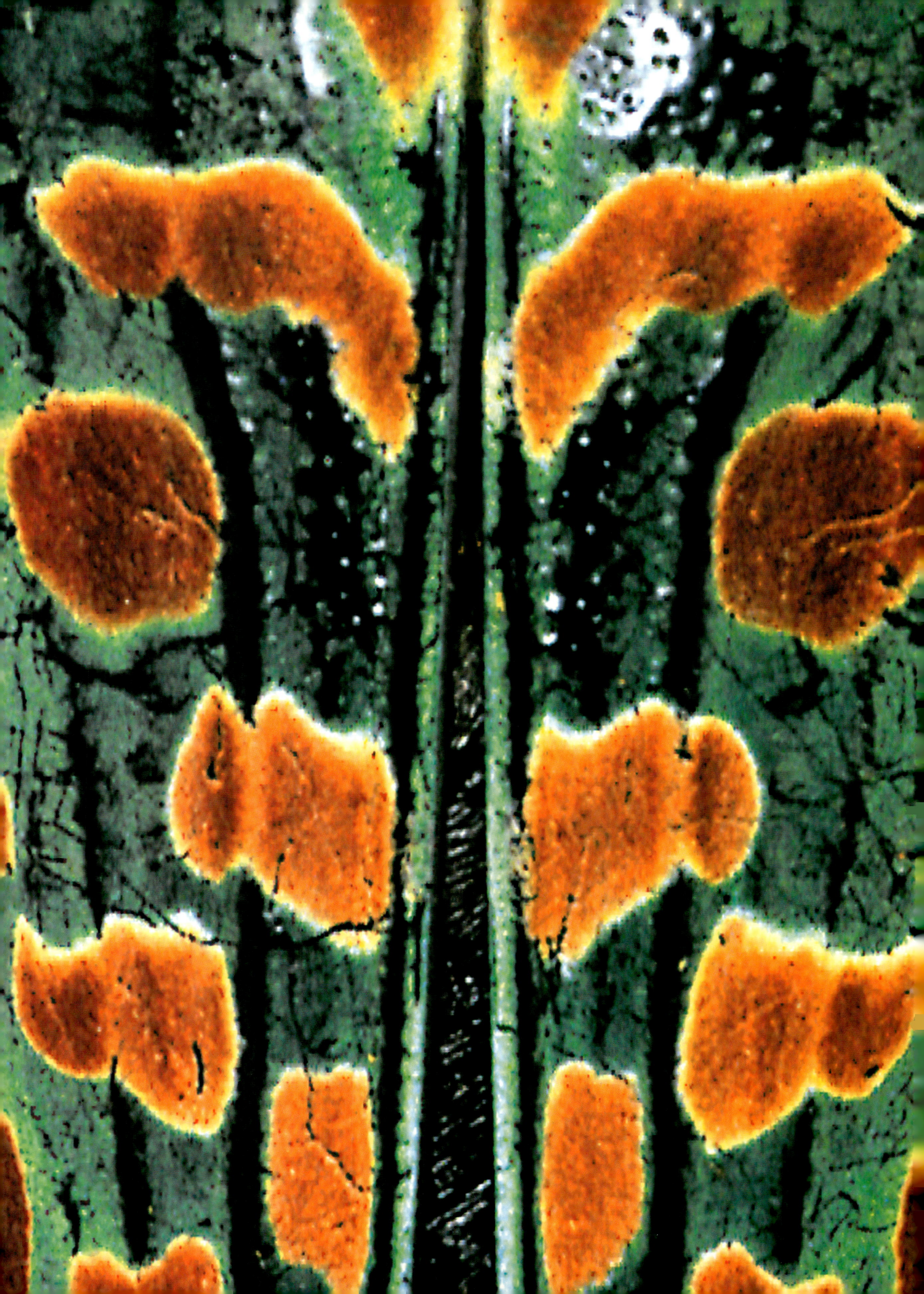

Sternotomis bohemani bohemani

Stellonatha maculata

Sternotomis variabilis

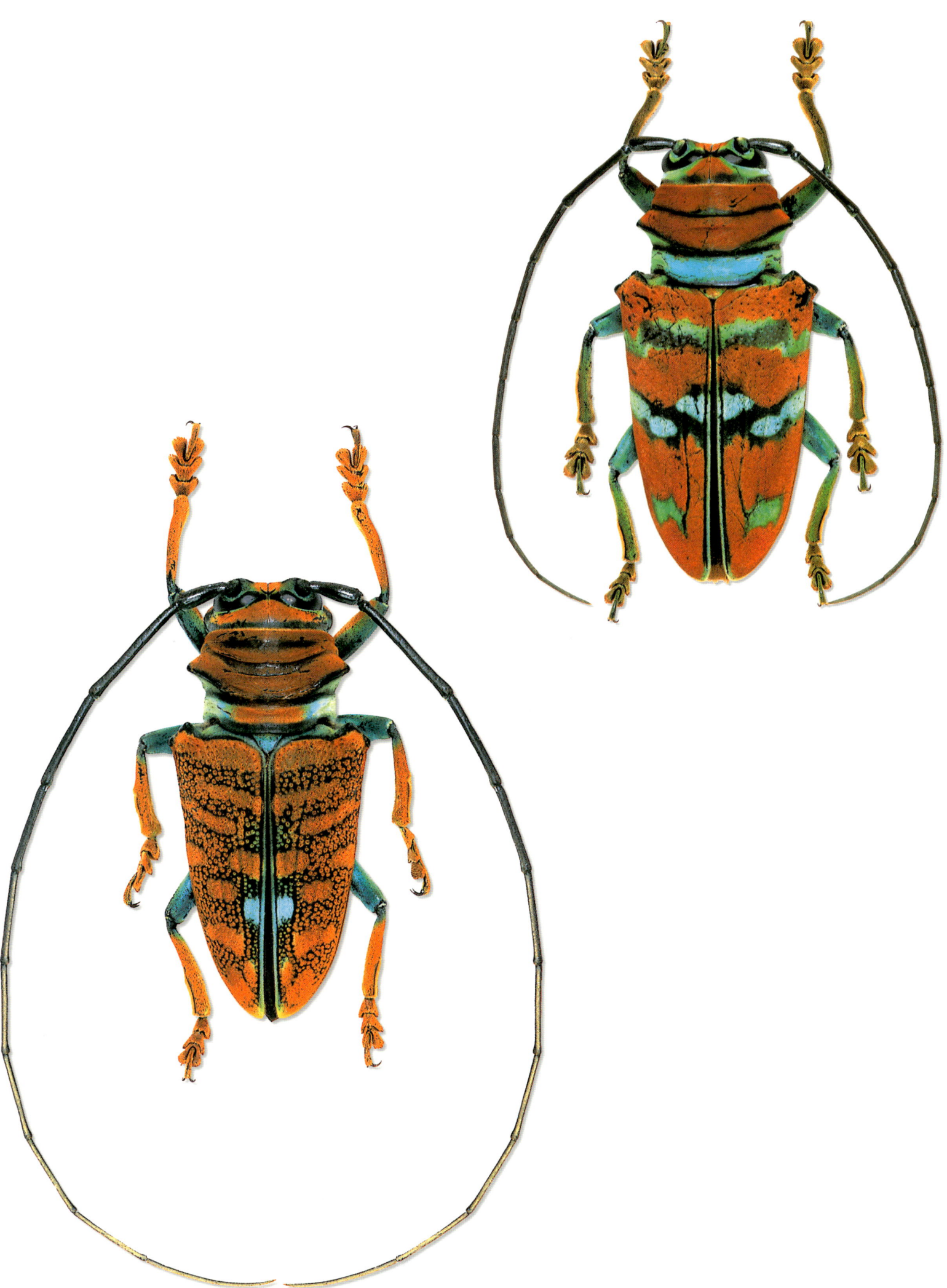

Sternotomis chrysopras reducta / Sternotomis pulchra picta

Sternotomis callais callais / Sternotomis callais bimaculata

26

Megacriodes saundersi

Calloplophora solli

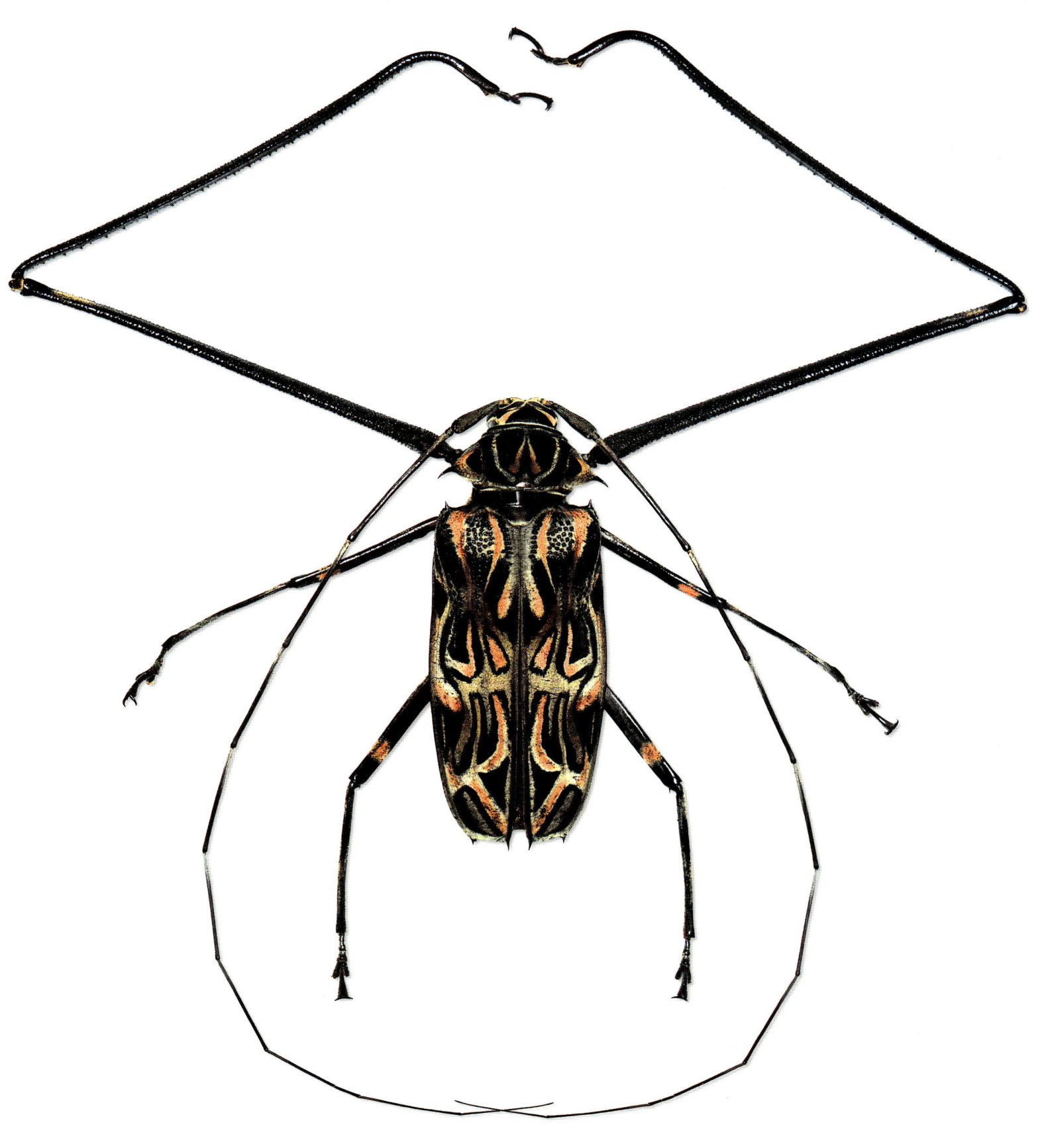

Acrocinus longimanus

Pachyteria dimidiata / Pachyteria equestris

30

Aristobia approximator

Plectrodera scalator

32

Batus barbicornis

Pavieia superba

Pseudomyagrus waterhousei

Rosenbergia straussi

Cheloderus childreni

Calostema sulphurea

Cerambycidae

39

Tragocephala crassicornis

40

Tragocephala guerini

41
Tragocephala nobilis ochracea

42

Polybothris sumptuosa gemma

Polybothris quadricollis

Chalcophora sp.

Lampropepla rothschildi

Iridotaenia chrysotoma

47

Chrysochroa raja assamensis

48

Euchroma gigantea

Julodis hiritiventris sanguinipilig

Sternocera hildebrandti

51
Chrysochroa purpureiventris

Belionota sumptuosa

Semiotus luteipennis

54
Semiotus ligneus

55
Chalcolepidius eschscholtzi

Chalcolepidius limbatus

57

Eupholus sp.

Eupholus sp.

Eupholus bennetti

60
Eupholus bennetti

61
Eupholus bennetti

Golofa pizarro

Eupatorus gracilicornis

Allomyrhina dichotomus taiwana

65

Xylotrupes gideon

Chrysina beyeri

Pelidnota aureocuprea

Pelidnota cyanipes

69

Chrysina karshi

Chrysina victorina

71

Chrysina boucardi

Pelidnota punctata

73
Chrysina gloriosa

74

Chrysocarabus auronitens

Mouhotia planipennis

Oxysternum conspicillatum

77

Phanaeus igneus floridanus

Phanaeus damon

79

Phanaeus damon

BEETLE PROFILES

Note: Size of beetles given is length from front of head to back of abdomen, excluding legs and antennae.

FLOWER BEETLES

are members of the family Scarabaeidae. The plates shown are all from the subfamily Cetoniinae. Species of this subfamily are sought after by collectors because of their striking patterns and colors. Most adult flower beetles feed on flower pollen, tree foliage, and fruit. Larvae feed primarily on plant roots or the organic material of decaying trees. Cetoniinae vary widely in size, coloration, and patterning. They have global distribution. As with all beetles, they are classified into families and subfamilies based on common structural features.

Plate 1
Stephanorrhina guttata
Family Scarabaeidae/Subfamily Cetoniinae
Location: Zaire/Size: 2.5 cm

Plate 2
Gymnetis hyperoglyphica obscura
Family Scarabaeidae/Subfamily Cetoniinae
Location: Panama/Size: 2 cm

Gymnetis flavomarginata sallei
Family Scarabaeidae/Subfamily Cetoniinae
Location: USA/Size: 2.5 cm

Plate 3
Euchroea histrionica
Family Scarabaeidae/Subfamily Cetoniinae
Location: Madagascar/Size: 2 cm

Plate 4
Gymnetis pantherina
Family Scarabaeidae/Subfamily Cetoniinae
Location: Venezuela/Size: 2 cm

Plate 5
Gymnetis flaveola
Family Scarabaeidae/Subfamily Cetoniinae
Location: Venezuela/Size: 2 cm

Rhomborrhina resplendens
Family Scarabaeidae/Subfamily Cetoniinae
Location: Thailand/Size: 2 cm

Plate 6
Gymnetis stellata
Family Scarabaeidae/Subfamily Cetoniinae
Location: Mexico/Size: 2 cm

Plate 7
Celedota splendens
Family Scarabaeidae/Subfamily Cetoniinae
Location: Madagascar/Size: 2 cm

Plate 8
Phaedimus jagori
Family Scarabaeidae/Subfamily Cetoniinae
Location: Philippines/Size: 2.3 cm

Plate 9
Theodosia perakensis
Family Scarabaeidae/Subfamily Cetoniinae
Location: Malaysia/Size: 3 cm

Plate 10
Euchroea clementi
Family Scarabaeidae/Subfamily Cetoniinae
Location: Madagascar/Size: 2.3 cm

Plate 11
Euchroea vadoni
Family Scarabaeidae/Subfamily Cetoniinae
Location: Madagascar/Size: 2 cm

Plate 12
Torynorrhina flammea
Family Scarabaeidae/Subfamily Cetoniinae
Location: Thailand/Size: 2 cm

Plate 13
Dicranorrhina derbyana
Family Scarabaeidae/Subfamily Cetoniinae
Location: Africa/Size: 5 cm

LONG-HORNED BEETLES

are members of the family Cerambycidae which includes many large subfamilies. All adult long-horned beetles feed on flower pollen, tree foliage, and fruit. Larvae feed primarily on plant roots or the organic material of living and decaying trees. The plates shown are from the three large subfamilies, Lepturninae (Flower Long-horned), Cerambycinae (Round-Necked Long-horned), and Lamiinae (Flat-Faced Long-horned). Many species of these families are favorites of collectors and bring high prices on the world market. Cerambycidae vary widely in size, coloration, patterning, and global distribution.

Plate 14
Steirastoma marmoratus
Family Cerambycidae/Subfamily Lamiinae
Location: Argentina/Size: 3 cm

Steirastoma brevis
Family Cerambycidae/Subfamily Lamiinae
Location: Bolivia/Size: 2.8 cm

Plate 15
Xylorhiza adusta
Family Cerambycidae/Subfamily Cerambycinae/Location: Malaysia/Size: 3 cm

Plate 16
Arrhenotus raphaelae
Family Cerambycidae/Subfamily Lamiinae
Location: Indonesia/Size: 2.3 cm

Plate 17
Euryphagus lundii
Family Cerambycidae/Subfamily Cerambycinae/Location: Java/Size: 2 cm

Plate 18
Rosalia alpina
Family Cerambycidae/Subfamily Cerambycinae/Location: Hungary/Size: 2.7 cm

Plate 19
Plinthocoelium suavoleus plicayum
Family Cerambycidae/Subfamily Cerambycinae/Location: USA/Size: 3.5 cm

Plate 20
Rhagium sycophanta
Family Cerambycidae/Subfamily Cerambycinae/Location: Europe/Size: 1.5 cm

Plate 21
Sternotomis bohemani bohemani
Family Cerambycidae/Subfamily Lamiinae
Location: South Africa/Size: 2 cm

Plate 22
Stellonatha maculata
Family Cerambycidae/Subfamily Lamiinae
Location: Madagascar/Size: 3 cm

Plate 23
Sternotomis variabilis
Family Cerambycidae/Subfamily Lamiinae
Location: Cameroon/Size: 2 cm

Plate 24
Sternotomis chrysopras reducta
Family Cerambycidae /Subfamily Lamiinae
Location: Cameroon/Size: 2.5 cm

Sternotomis pulchra picta
Family Cerambycidae/Subfamily Lamiinae
Location: Cameroon/Size: 2.5 cm

Plate 25
Sternotomis callais callais
Family Cerambycidae/Subfamily Lamiinae
Location: Cameroon/Size: 2 cm

Sternotomis callais bimaculata
Family Cerambycidae/Subfamily Lamiinae
Location: Gabon/Size: 2 cm

Plate 26
Megacriodes saundersi
Family Cerambycidae/Subfamily Cerambycinae/Location: Borneo/Size: 3 cm

Plate 27
Calloplophora solli
Family Cerambycidae/Subfamily Lamiinae
Location: Thailand/Size: 3 cm

Plate 28
Acrocinus longimanus
Family Cerambycidae/Subfamily Lamiinae
Location: Peru/Size: 5.5 cm

Plate 29
Pachyteria dimidiata
Family Cerambycidae/Subfamily Cerambycinae/Location: Malaysia/Size: 3 cm

Pachyteria equestris
Family Cerambycidae/Subfamily Cerambycinae/Location: Malaysia/Size: 3 cm

Plate 30
Aristobia approximator
Family Cerambycidae/Subfamily Lamiinae
Location: Thailand/Size: 3.2 cm

Plate 31
Plectrodera scalator
Family Cerambycidae/Subfamily Cerambycinae/Location: USA/Size: 3 cm

Plate 32
Batus barbicornis
Family Cerambycidae/Subfamily Lamiinae
Location: Guyana/Size: 3.5 cm

Plate 33
Pavieia superba
Family Cerambycidae/Subfamily Cerambycinae/Location: Thailand/Size: 3 cm

Plate 34
Pseudomyagrus waterhousei
Family Cerambycidae/Subfamily Cerambycinae/Location: Malaysia/Size: 1.5 cm

Plate 35
Rosenbergia straussi
Family Cerambycidae/Subfamily Lamiinae
Location: Papua New Guinea/Size: 4 cm

Plate 36
Cheloderus childreni
Family Cerambycidae/Subfamily Prioninae
Location: Chile/Size: 2.5 cm

Plate 37
Calostema sulphurea
Family Cerambycidae/Subfamily Lamiinae
Location: Thailand/Size: 3.7 cm

Plate 38
Family Cerambycidae/Subfamily Cerambycinae/Size: 2.7 cm

Plate 39
Tragocephala crassicornis
Family Cerambycidae/Subfamily Lamiinae
Location: Africa/Size: 2.6 cm

Plate 40
Tragocephala guerini
Family Cerambycidae/Subfamily Lamiinae
Location: Africa/Size: 2.7 cm

Plate 41
Tragocephala nobilis ochracea
Family Cerambycidae/Subfamily Lamiinae
Location: Africa/Size: 2.7 cm

METALLIC WOOD-BORING BEETLES
are members of the family Buprestidae. Most adult metallic beetles feed on flower pollen, tree foliage, and fruit. Larvae feed primarily on plant roots or the organic material of decaying trees. Buprestidae vary widely in size, coloration, patterning, and global distribution. Members of this family are usually shiny and nearly always metallic in color. Species of this family are some of the most prized by collectors because of their jewel-like beauty.

Plate 42
Polybothris sumptuosa gemma
Family Buprestidae/Location: Madagascar
Size: 3.4 cm

Plate 43
Polybothris quadricollis
Family Buprestidae/Location: Madagascar
Size: 3.7 cm

Plate 44
Chalcophora sp.
Family Buprestidae/Size: 2.5 cm

Plate 45
Lampropepla rothschildi
Family Buprestidae/Location: Madagascar
Size: 3.5 cm

Plate 46
Iridotaenia chrysotoma
Family Buprestidae/Location: Thailand
Size: 2 cm

Plate 47
Chrysochroa raja assamensis
Family Buprestidae/Location: Thailand
Size: 3.2 cm

Plate 48
Euchroma gigantea
Family Buprestidae/Location: Latin America/Size: 5 cm

Plate 49
Julodis hiritiventris sanguinipilig
Family Buprestidae/Location: South Africa
Size: 2 cm

Plate 50
Sternocera hildebrandti
Family Buprestidae/Location: Africa
Size: 3.8 cm

Plate 51
Chrysochroa purpureiventris
Family Buprestidae/Location: Thailand
Size: 4 cm

Plate 52
Belionota sumptuosa
Family Buprestidae/Location: Thailand
Size: 2 cm

CLICK BEETLES
are members of the family Elateridae. Most adults feed on tree foliage and bushes. Larvae feed primarily on plant roots. Click beetles have a mechanism which allows them to contract their bodies and flip into the air in order to right themselves if they are stranded on their backs. This action produces a loud click. Snapjacks and skipjacks are also common names given to this family. Click beetles vary widely in size, coloration, patterning, and global distribution.

Plate 53
Semiotus luteipennis
Family Elateridae/Location: Chile
Size: 3 cm

Plate 54
Semiotus ligneus
Family Elateridae/Location: Bolivia
Size: 2.7 cm

Plate 55
Chalcolepidius eschscholtzi
Family Elateridae/Location: Latin America/Size: 3 cm

Plate 56
Chalcolepidius limbatus
Family Elateridae/Location: Argentina
Size: 3 cm

WEEVIL BEETLES
are members of the superfamily Curculionoidea, which contains many very large families and subfamilies. Adult weevil beetles feed on flower pollen, tree foliage, and fruit. Larvae feed primarily on plant roots or the organic material of decaying trees. All the plates here are from the family Curculionidae, and the subfamily Curculioninae which boasts some of the most outstanding patterning and coloration. Curculionidae vary widely in size, coloration, patterning, and global distribution. The Curculionoidea superfamily has the largest number of species of any family in the animal kingdom.

Plates 57 and 58
Eupholus sp.
Family Curculionidae/Subfamily Curculioninae/Location: Papua New Guinea
Size: 2.3 cm

Plate 59
Eupholus bennetti
Family Curculionidae/Subfamily Curculioninae/Location: Papua New Guinea
Size: 2.4 cm

Plates 60 and 61
Eupholus bennetti
Family Curculionidae/Subfamily Curculioninae/Location: Papua New Guinea
Size: 2.3 cm

RHINOCEROS BEETLES
are members of the family Scarabaeidae, and very large subfamily Dynastinae. Other common names are hercules and elephant beetles. Most adult rhinoceros beetles feed on tree foliage. Larvae feed primarily on plant roots. Dynastinae vary widely in global distribution and size but have little variation in coloration and patterning. Most species of this subfamily have horns and are some of the largest beetles.

Plate 62
Golofa pizarro
Family Scarabaeidae/Subfamily Dynastinae
Location: Mexico/Size: 4.5 cm

Plate 63
Eupatorus gracilicornis
Family Scarabaeidae/Subfamily Dynastinae
Location: Malaysia/Size: 5.5 cm

Plate 64
Allomyrhina dichotomus taiwana
Family Scarabaeidae/Subfamily Dynastinae
Location: Taiwan/Size: 5 cm

Plate 65
Xylotrupes gideon
Family Scarabaeidae/Subfamily Dynastinae
Location: Thailand/Size: 5.3 cm

SHINING LEAF BEETLES
are members of the family Scarabaeidae, and large subfamily Rutelinae. Most adults feed on tree foliage and fruit. Larvae feed primarily on plant roots. Due to their striking coloration and precision, machine-like armor plating, members of this subfamily are becoming the most sought after by collectors. Rutelinae vary widely in size, coloration, patterning, and global distribution.

Plate 66
Chrysina beyeri
Family Scarabaeidae/Subfamily Rutelinae
Location: USA/Size: 2.4 cm

Plate 67
Pelidnota aureocuprea
Family Scarabaeidae/Subfamily Rutelinae
Location: Venezuela/Size: 2 cm

Plate 68
Pelidnota cyanipes
Family Scarabaeidae/Subfamily Rutelinae
Location: Brazil/Size: 3 cm

Plate 69
Chrysina karshi
Family Scarabaeidae/Subfamily Rutelinae
Location: Guatemala/Size: 2.7 cm

Plate 70
Chrysina victorina
Family Scarabaeidae/Subfamily Rutelinae
Location: Mexico/Size: 3.2 cm

Plate 71
Chrysina boucardi
Family Scarabaeidae/Subfamily Rutelinae
Location: Costa Rica/Size: 2.6 cm

Plate 72
Pelidnota punctata
Family Scarabaeidae/Subfamily Rutelinae
Location: USA/Size: 2.6 cm

Plates 73
Chrysina gloriosa
Family Scarabaeidae/Subfamily Rutelinae
Location: USA/Size: 2 cm

GROUND BEETLES are members of the family Carabidae which includes many subfamilies. Adults and larvae feed on dead or dying insects, some preying on living insects. Carabidae vary widely in size, coloration, patterning, and global distribution. As their name implies, these beetles live on the ground.

Plate 74
Chrysocarabus auronitens
Family Carabidae/Location: Europe
Size: 2.5 cm

Plate 75
Mouhotia planipennis
Family Carabidae/Location: Thailand
Size: 2 cm

DUNG BEETLES are members of the family Scarabaeidae, and very large subfamily Scarabaeinae. Most of the adult and larval dung beetles feed on dung. Scarabaeinae vary widely in size, coloration, patterning, and global distribution.

Plate 76
Oxysternum conspicillatum
Family Scarabaeidae/Subfamily Scarabaeinae/Location: Venezuela
Size: 2.4 cm

Plate 77
Phanaeus igneus floridanus
Family Scarabaeidae/Subfamily Scarabaeinae/Location: USA
Size: 2 cm

Plates 78 and 79
Phanaeus damon
Family Scarabaeidae/Subfamily Scarabaeinae/Location: Nicaragua
Size: 2 cm

(Plate 38 has only been identified to the family level.)

SELECTED BIBLIOGRAPHY

Evans, Arthur V., and Charles L. Bellamy. 1996. *An Inordinate Fondness for Beetles*. Berkeley and Los Angeles: University of California Press.

Evans, Glyn. 1975. *The Life of Beetles*. New York: Hafner.

Fabre, J. Henri. 1918. *The Sacred Beetle and Others*. New York: Dodd, Mead.

Klausnitzer, Bernhard. 1981. *Beetles*. New York: Exeter.

Nissenson, Marilyn, and Susan Jonas. 2000. *Jeweled Bugs and Butterflies*. New York: Abrams.

Ohmomo, Sadahiro, and Koyo Akiyama.1997. *Jewel Beetles*. Tokyo: E S I.

Reitter, Ewald. 1961. *Beetles*. London: Hamlyn.

Simon, Hilda. 1971. *The Splendor of Iridescence: Structural Colors in the Animal World*. New York: Dodd, Mead & Company.

SOURCES ON THE WORLD WIDE WEB
http://www.living-jewels.com
Authors Poul Beckmann and Ruth Kaspin offer general information on beetles, links, and more extraordinary insect images.

Beetle Breeding Web Page
http://www.dorcus.com/
Author Fan Lin presents information on rearing stag, rhinoceros, and flower beetles. The site features an extensive photo library including a "beetle of the month." The site has English and Japanese language versions.

Stag Beetles of Taiwan
http://www.geocities.com/RainForest/1803/stag.htm
This site contains information on beetle breeding, proper care of pet beetles, and collecting and curating of specimens.

Slovak Beetles Friends
http://www.setcom.sk/
Author Milan Polaczyk presents beetle breeding information and offers beetle larvae for sale and trade.

Ookuwagata
http://www.kakaa.or.jp/~isobe/ookuwa/manual/english.htm
Author Kameari Kabuto has created the definitive online manual detailing the care of Ookuwagata, Japan's most popular beetle pet. Posted in English and Japanese language versions, this site offers the most specific treatment of stag beetle care.

Japanese Stag Beetle
http://www.sm.rim.or.jp/~tanida/stagbeetle.html
Author Kouichi Tanida offers beetle collecting and breeding information, photo galleries, and links to other beetle hobbyists.

Elytra and Antenna: US Insects
http://www.geocities.com/Heartland/Park/2638/
This site features brief profiles of beetles native to the United States, photographs of adult and immature phases, and rearing information.

http://www.jollyroger.com/library/TheAutobiographyofCharlesDarwinebook.html
From *The Life and Letters of Charles Darwin*, edited by his Son Francis Darwin.

http://www.bugbios.com/ced2/beetles_tex.html
Rivers, Victoria Z., "Beetles in Textiles" in *Cultural Entomology Digest*, issue 2, February 1994.

http://www.bugbios.com/ced2/beetles_rel_sym.html
Cambefort, Yves, "Beetles As Religious Symbols" in *Cultural Entomology Digest* issue 2, February 1994.